the BREAD MACHINE BOOK

Simple and delicious recipes for breads, cakes,
pizzas and pastries, at the touch of a button.

LINDA DOESER

This is a Parragon Book
First published in 2002

Parragon
Queen Street House
4 Queen Street
Bath BA1 1HE, UK

Produced by The Bridgewater Book Company Ltd

Photographer **Calvey Taylor-Haw**
Home economist **Michaela Jester**

Hardback ISBN: 0-75259-189-4
Paperback ISBN:0-75259-336-6

Printed in China

Notes

• This book uses both metric and imperial measurements. Follow
the same units of measurement throughout; do not mix metric
and imperial.

• All spoon measurements are level: teaspoons are assumed to be 5 ml
and tablespoons are assumed to be 15 ml.

CONTENTS

INTRODUCTION

There can be few more appetising aromas than the smell of bread baking and few more delicious tastes than a still-warm, freshly cooked loaf. With a bread machine, this can quickly become a trouble-free, everyday treat. If you have a timer delay, fresh bread every morning is even less bother than brewing a pot of coffee.

The recipes in this book cover all kinds of bread for every occasion and lifestyle. There are simple, basic breads that require no more effort than measuring a few ingredients into the machine and pressing the start switch, yet even these provide a wide range of flavours, from a plain white loaf to a moist fruit bread. More ambitious cooks can use the bread machine to take the hard work out of making the dough, and create professional-looking plaits, baguettes, baps, breadsticks and Danish pastries. The bread machine's versatility is further explored with mouthwatering pizza recipes, as well as some fabulous cakes to perk up mid-morning coffee or afternoon tea.

ABOUT BREAD MACHINES

Although a bread machine is easy to use it must be treated with care. Here are some tips for working a bread machine for the best results.

Make sure that the kneading blade is firmly attached. Do not plug the machine in until you are ready to switch it on. Always remove the bread pan to add the ingredients to avoid spills inside the machine.

Add the ingredients in the order listed unless instructed otherwise. Measure ingredients accurately.

Add ingredients such as eggs at room temperature. Use hand-hot liquid – but no hotter – as this will activate the yeast. Make sure that flours and yeast are not past their 'use-by' dates.

Do not open the bread machine during cooking, except when necessary for adding extra ingredients, such as dried fruit. Otherwise, the temperature will drop and the bread will be disappointing.

Use oven gloves to remove the bread pan after baking – it will be very hot. Make sure the bread machine is on a level surface and cannot be reached by young children.

Do not use the timer delay for recipes that include perishable ingredients, such as eggs, yogurt or buttermilk.

The recipes have been tested in medium-sized machines. They are all suitable for large machines and most will work successfully in small machines. Check the manufacturer's handbook for maximum capacity.

For shaped loaves, follow the instructions for proving the dough (letting it rise). Put in a warm place, such as an airing cupboard. The dough may take longer to rise in a cooler place. If you need to use a conventional oven, preheat the oven fully before baking.

The kneading blade should be well-seated in the bottom of the bread pan.

Make sure that you add the ingredients in the order given by the recipe.

Check that the bread pan is sitting securely in the machine before kneading begins.

BASIC BREADS

Here are easy recipes for a wide range of basic breads. For the simplest you just add the ingredients to the bread machine, press start, and turn out a perfect loaf to cool. Varying the ingredients produces a delicious selection of breads, from a healthy Harvest Loaf to a tasty Corn Bread. There are also popular breads and rolls such as White Baps and Pittas for cooking in a conventional oven. Use the bread machine to make perfect dough, then turn out and shape before baking. You will find that more specialist breads, such as Plaited Poppy Seed Bread and Baguettes, are well within the scope of the beginner.

CRUSTY LOAF

INGREDIENTS
1 egg
1 egg yolk
hand-hot water, as required
500 g/1 lb 2 oz strong white
    bread flour
1½ tsp salt
2 tsp sugar
25 g /1 oz butter, softened or diced
1 tsp easy-blend dried yeast

1 Remove the bread pan from the bread machine. Put the egg and egg yolk into a measuring jug and beat lightly to mix; then add sufficient hand-hot water to make up to 300 ml/10 fl oz. Stir to mix. Pour into the bread pan.

2 Sprinkle the flour over the liquid so that it is completely covered. Place the salt, sugar and butter in 3 corners of the pan. Make an indentation in the flour with your finger without exposing the liquid and add the yeast to it.

3 Fit the bread pan in the machine and close the lid. Set the bread machine to the basic setting, medium crust, and press start.

4 When the cycle has finished, switch off the machine. Remove the bread pan with oven gloves and turn out the bread on to a wire rack to cool. Remove the kneading blade, if necessary.

MILK BREAD

INGREDIENTS

200 ml/7 fl oz hand-hot full cream
   or semi-skimmed milk
100 ml/3½ fl oz hand-hot water
450 g/1 lb strong white bread flour

1½ tsp salt
2 tsp sugar
25 g/1 oz butter, softened or diced
1 tsp easy-blend dried yeast

1 Remove the bread pan from the bread machine. Pour the milk and water into the bread pan.

2 Sprinkle the flour over the liquid so that it is completely covered. Place the salt, sugar and butter in 3 corners of the pan. Make an indentation in the flour with your finger without exposing the liquid and add the yeast to it.

3 Fit the bread pan in the machine and close the lid. Set the bread machine to the basic setting, medium crust, and press start.

4 When the cycle has finished, switch off the machine. Remove the bread pan with oven gloves and turn out the bread on to a wire rack to cool. Remove the kneading blade, if necessary.

HARVEST LOAF

INGREDIENTS
175 ml/6 fl oz hand-hot water
1½ tbsp sunflower oil
225 g/8 oz strong wholemeal
    bread flour
1 tbsp skimmed milk powder
1 tsp salt
2 tbsp soft brown sugar
1 tsp easy-blend dried yeast

1 Remove the bread pan from the bread machine. Pour the water into the bread pan and add the sunflower oil.

2 Sprinkle the flour over the liquid so that it is completely covered, then sprinkle in the skimmed milk powder. Place the salt and sugar in 2 corners of the pan. Make an indentation in the flour with your finger without exposing the liquid and add the yeast to it.

3 Fit the bread pan in the machine and close the lid. Set the bread machine to the wholemeal setting, medium crust, and press start.

4 When the cycle has finished, switch off the machine. Remove the bread pan with oven gloves and turn out the bread on to a wire rack to cool. Remove the kneading blade, if necessary.

CORN BREAD

INGREDIENTS
150 ml/5 fl oz hand-hot water
5 tbsp hand-hot milk
1 tbsp corn oil
280 g/10 oz strong white bread flour
100 g/3½ oz fine cornmeal
1 tsp salt
1½ tsp light brown sugar
1 tsp easy-blend dried yeast

Topping
1 tbsp water
1 tbsp medium cornmeal

1 Remove the bread pan from the bread machine. Pour in the water, milk and corn oil.

2 Sprinkle the flour over the liquid so that it is completely covered, then sprinkle in the cornmeal. Place the salt and sugar in 2 corners of the pan. Make an indentation in the flour with your finger without exposing the liquid and add the yeast to it.

3 Fit the bread pan in the machine and close the lid. Set the bread machine to the quick setting, medium crust, and press start. About 5 minutes before baking begins (about 20 minutes from the start), add the topping. Brush the top of the dough with the water and carefully sprinkle with the medium cornmeal.

4 When the cycle has finished, switch off the machine. Remove the bread pan with oven gloves and turn out the bread on to a wire rack to cool. Remove the kneading blade if necessary.

WHITE BAPS

INGREDIENTS
140 ml/4½ fl oz hand-hot water
140 ml/4½ fl oz hand-hot milk
450 g/1 lb strong white bread flour,
    plus extra for dusting
1½ tsp salt
2 tsp caster sugar
1 tsp easy-blend dried yeast
sunflower oil, for greasing
milk, for glazing

1 Remove the bread pan from the bread machine. Pour the water and milk into the bread pan. Sprinkle the flour over the liquid so that it is completely covered. Place the salt and sugar in 2 corners of the pan. Make an indentation in the flour with your finger without exposing the liquid and add the yeast to it.

2 Fit the bread pan in the machine and close the lid. Set the bread machine to the dough setting and press start.

3 When the cycle has finished, switch off the machine and remove the bread pan. Lightly flour a work surface and remove the dough from the pan. Knock back gently, then divide it into 10 equal pieces. Place on a tray and cover with lightly oiled clingfilm.

4 Lightly oil 2 baking sheets. Take a piece of dough from underneath the clingfilm, shape it into a ball, then place on a lightly floured surface and roll out into a 10-cm/4-inch-long oval. Roll out the other pieces in the same way, place on the baking sheets and cover with lightly oiled clingfilm. Set aside in a warm place for 30 minutes to rise.

5 Remove the clingfilm and gently press the centre of each bap with 2 fingers to release any large air bubbles, then brush the tops with milk and dust with a little flour. Bake in a preheated oven, 200°C/400°F/Gas Mark 6, for 15–20 minutes, until lightly browned. Transfer the baps to wire racks to cool slightly. Serve warm.

BAGUETTES

INGREDIENTS
325 ml/11 fl oz hand-hot water
450 g/1 lb strong white bread flour,
    plus extra for dusting
1½ tsp salt
1½ tsp easy-blend dried yeast
sunflower oil, for greasing

1 Remove the bread pan from the bread machine. Pour the water into the bread pan. Sprinkle the flour over the liquid so that it is completely covered. Place the salt in 1 corner of the pan. Make an indentation in the flour with your finger without exposing the liquid and add the yeast to it.

2 Fit the bread pan in the machine and close the lid. Set the bread machine to the French dough setting and press start. If your machine has only a French bread baking setting, remove the dough after the final rising (about 2 hours and 55 minutes from the start).

3 When the cycle has finished, switch off the machine and remove the bread pan. Lightly flour a work surface and remove the dough from the pan. Knock back, then divide into 2 equal pieces. Shape each piece into a ball, then roll out each ball to a 20 x 7.5-cm/8 x 3-inch rectangle. With the long side of a rectangle facing you, fold the top third of dough down and the bottom third up and press together. Set aside to rest while you fold the second rectangle. Then repeat twice more with each rectangle, leaving them to rest in between each folding.

4 Lightly flour and pleat 2 tea towels. Gently roll and stretch each piece of dough, in turn, into a stick about 30 cm/12 inches long. Place each baguette between the pleats of a tea towel to support it and cover with lightly oiled clingfilm. Set aside in a warm place for 30–40 minutes to rise.

5 Lightly oil a baking sheet. Remove the clingfilm and gently roll the loaves from the tea towels on to the baking sheet, spaced well apart. Make several diagonal slashes on the tops, with a sharp knife. Set the oven at 230°C/450°F/Gas Mark 8. Spray the preheated oven with water and bake the loaves for 15–20 minutes, until crusty and golden. Transfer to a wire rack to cool.

BREADSTICKS WITH SESAME SEEDS

INGREDIENTS

200 ml/7 fl oz hand-hot water

3 tbsp olive oil, plus extra for greasing
and brushing

350 g/12 oz strong white bread flour,
plus extra for dusting

1½ tsp salt

1½ tsp easy-blend dried yeast

sesame seeds, for coating

1 Remove the bread pan from the bread machine. Pour the water into the bread pan and add the olive oil. Sprinkle the flour over the liquid so that it is completely covered. Place the salt in 1 corner of the bread pan. Make an indentation in the flour with your finger without exposing the liquid and add the yeast to it.

2 Fit the bread pan in the machine and close the lid. Set the bread machine to the dough setting and press start.

3 When the cycle has finished, switch off the machine and remove the bread pan. Lightly flour a work surface and remove the dough from the pan. Knock back and roll out to a 23 x 20-cm/9 x 8-inch rectangle. Cut the dough into 3 strips, each 20 cm/8 inches long, then cut each strip across into 10 equal pieces.

4 Gently roll and stretch each piece of dough into a stick about 30 cm/12 inches long. Lightly oil 2 baking sheets. Spread out the sesame seeds on a large, shallow plate or tray. Roll each breadstick in the sesame seeds to coat, then place on the baking sheets, spaced well apart. Brush with olive oil, cover with clingfilm and set aside in a warm place for 15 minutes.

5 Remove the clingfilm and bake the breadsticks in a preheated oven, 200°C/400°F/Gas Mark 6, for 10 minutes. Turn them over, return to the oven and bake for a further 5–10 minutes, until golden. Transfer to a wire rack to cool.

PITTAS

INGREDIENTS
210 ml/7½ fl oz hand-hot water
350 g/12 oz strong white bread flour,
    plus extra for dusting
1½ tsp salt
1 tsp sugar
1 tsp easy-blend dried yeast
1 tbsp olive oil, plus extra for greasing

1 Remove the bread pan from the bread machine and pour in the water and the olive oil. Sprinkle the flour over the liquid so that it is completely covered. Place the salt and sugar in 2 corners of the pan. Make an indentation in the flour with your finger without exposing the liquid and add the yeast to it.

2 Fit the bread pan in the machine and close the lid. Set the bread machine to the pizza dough setting and press start. (If your machine does not have a pizza dough setting, refer to the manufacturer's handbook to check whether you should use the dough setting or the cake setting. If using the cake setting, switch off the machine at the end of the final rising – about 1 hour and 40 minutes from the start.)

3 When the cycle has finished, switch off the machine and remove the bread pan. Lightly oil a baking sheet. Lightly flour a work surface and remove the dough from the pan. Knock back gently, then divide into 6 equal pieces. Shape each piece into a ball and place on the baking sheet. Cover with oiled clingfilm and set aside for 10 minutes. Meanwhile, place 2 or 3 baking sheets in the oven and preheat to 230°C/450°F/Gas Mark 8.

4 Uncover the dough and flatten each piece slightly. Roll out each piece on a lightly floured surface into a round. Sprinkle lightly with flour and cover with clingfilm. Set aside for a further 10 minutes to rest. Remove the clingfilm. Transfer the dough rounds to the hot baking sheets, spaced well apart, and bake for 5 minutes, until risen and golden. Transfer to a wire rack to cool.

PLAITED POPPY SEED BREAD

INGREDIENTS

175 ml/6 fl oz hand-hot water

2 tbsp sunflower oil, plus extra
  for greasing

225 g/8 oz strong white bread flour,
  plus extra for dusting

2 tbsp skimmed milk powder

1 tsp salt

1¹/₄ tbsp sugar

1 tsp easy-blend dried yeast

3 tbsp poppy seeds

Topping

1 egg yolk

1 tbsp milk

1 tbsp caster sugar

2 tbsp poppy seeds

1 Remove the bread pan from the bread machine. Pour in the water and add the sunflower oil. Sprinkle the flour over the liquid so that it is completely covered, then sprinkle in the skimmed milk powder. Place the salt and sugar in 2 corners of the pan. Make an indentation in the flour with your finger without exposing the liquid and add the yeast to it.

2 Fit the bread pan in the machine and close the lid. Set the bread machine to the dough setting and press start. When the machine beeps for extra ingredients, or 5 minutes before the end of kneading, add the poppy seeds.

3 When the cycle has finished, switch off the machine and remove the bread pan. Lightly flour a work surface and remove the dough from the pan. Knock back gently and knead lightly for 1–2 minutes.

4 Oil a baking sheet. Divide the dough into 3 equal pieces and shape each piece into a rope about 25–30 cm/10–12 inches long. Place the ropes side by side and pinch them together at one end. Plait the

dough, and pinch the other end together, tucking it underneath. Place the plait on the baking sheet, cover with lightly oiled clingfilm and set aside in a warm place for about 30 minutes to rise.

5 To make the topping, lightly beat the egg yolk with the milk and caster sugar to combine. Remove the clingfilm from the plait, brush the top with the egg glaze and sprinkle over the poppy seeds. Bake in a preheated oven, 200°C/400°F/Gas Mark 6, for 30–35 minutes, until the loaf is golden and sounds hollow when tapped. Transfer to a wire rack to cool.

BREAKFAST BRIOCHE

INGREDIENTS
2 eggs, at room temperature
2 tbsp hand-hot milk
225 g/8 oz strong white bread flour,
    plus extra for dusting
½ tsp salt
1 tbsp caster sugar
55 g/2 oz butter, melted
1½ tsp easy-blend dried yeast
sunflower oil, for greasing

Glaze
1 egg yolk
1 tbsp milk or water

1 Remove the bread pan from the bread machine. Lightly beat the eggs with the milk in a bowl, then pour into the bread pan. Sprinkle the flour over the liquid so that it is completely covered. Place the salt, sugar and melted butter in 3 corners of the pan. Make an indentation in the flour with your finger without exposing the liquid and add the yeast to it.

2 Fit the bread pan in the machine and close the lid. Set the bread machine to the dough setting and press start. When the cycle has finished, switch off the machine. Leave the dough in the machine, with the lid shut, for an extra 30 minutes, or until the dough is well risen.

3 Remove the bread pan. Lightly flour a work surface and remove the dough from the pan. Knock back gently. Slice off one-quarter of the dough, wrap in

oiled clingfilm and set aside. Oil a brioche mould. Knead the large piece of dough lightly and shape into a ball. Place in the mould and make an indentation or cut a cross in the top with a sharp knife. Unwrap and lightly knead the reserved dough, shape into a round, then elongate slightly to a rough pear shape. Place the pear-shaped dough on top of the larger ball of dough, narrow end downwards. Cover with lightly oiled clingfilm and set aside in a warm place for about 1 hour to rise.

4 Remove the clingfilm. To make the glaze, lightly beat the egg yolk with the milk, then brush over the top of the brioche. Bake in a preheated oven, 220˚C/425˚F/Gas Mark 7, for 40–45 minutes, until risen and golden. Transfer to a wire rack to cool. Serve warm or cold.

HEALTHY SNACKS

These substantial flavour-packed loaves provide a delicious and healthy snack. They also add the perfect touch to a picnic, lunch or party. Potatoes, cheese and yogurt can all be easily incorporated into the dough to create loaves such as Oatmeal and Potato Bread, Cheesy Chive Granary Bread or Wholemeal Yogurt Bread, which will liven up any meal. Naan with coriander is an excellent addition to a main course if you are preparing a curry, but it can also be baked as a lunchtime snack as an alternative to rolls or loaves.

OATMEAL AND POTATO BREAD

INGREDIENTS

225 g/8 oz floury potatoes
  (peeled weight)
210 ml/7½ fl oz hand-hot water
500 g/1 lb 2 oz strong white
  bread flour
3 tbsp rolled oats
2 tbsp skimmed milk powder
1½ tsp salt

1½ tbsp dark brown sugar
40 g/1½ oz butter, softened
  or diced
1½ tsp easy-blend dried yeast

Topping
1 tbsp water
1 tbsp rolled oats

1 Place the potatoes in a large pan, add water to cover, bring to the boil and cook for 20–25 minutes, until tender. Drain, then mash until smooth. Cool.

2 Remove the bread pan from the bread machine. Pour in the water. Sprinkle the flour over the liquid so that it is covered, then sprinkle in the oats and milk powder. Add the mashed potatoes to the bread pan, then place the salt, sugar and butter in 3 corners of the pan. Make an indention in the flour with your finger without exposing the liquid and add the yeast to it.

3 Fit the bread pan in the machine and close the lid. Set the bread machine to the basic setting, medium crust, and press start. About 5 minutes before the end of the final rising cycle (about 1¼ hours from the start), add the topping. Brush the surface of the loaf with the water and carefully sprinkle over the rolled oats.

4 When the cycle has finished, switch off the machine. Remove the bread pan with oven gloves and turn out the bread on to a wire rack to cool. Remove the kneading blade if necessary.

RYE AND SEED BREAD

INGREDIENTS
360 ml/12½ fl oz hand-hot water
2 tbsp sunflower oil
2½ tbsp treacle
250 g/9 oz strong white bread flour
140 g/5 oz rye flour
85 g/3 oz wholemeal flour
75 g/2¾ oz dried breadcrumbs
3 tbsp oat bran
1½ tsp salt
1½ tbsp cocoa powder
2 tsp caraway seeds
½ tsp easy-blend dried yeast

1 Remove the bread pan from the bread machine. Pour the water into the bread pan and add the oil and treacle.

2 Sprinkle all 3 types of flour over the liquid so that it is completely covered, then sprinkle in the breadcrumbs and oat bran. Place the salt, cocoa powder and caraway seeds in 3 corners of the pan. Make an indentation in the flour with your finger without exposing the liquid and add the yeast to it.

3 Fit the bread pan in the machine and close the lid. Set the bread machine to the wholemeal setting, medium crust, and press start.

4 When the cycle has finished, switch off the machine. Remove the bread pan with oven gloves and turn out the bread on to a wire rack to cool. Remove the kneading blade if necessary.

WHOLEMEAL YOGURT BREAD

INGREDIENTS

150 ml/5 fl oz hand-hot water

125 ml/4 fl oz natural yogurt, at
    room temperature

1 tbsp sunflower oil

1 tbsp treacle or golden syrup

200 g/7 oz strong white bread flour

150 g/5½ oz strong wholemeal
    bread flour

25 g/1 oz wheat bran

1 tsp salt

¾ tsp easy-blend dried yeast

1 Remove the bread pan from the bread machine. Pour in the water and add the yogurt, sunflower oil and treacle.

2 Sprinkle both types of flour over the liquid so that it is completely covered. Place the wheat bran and salt in 2 corners of the pan. Make an indentation in the flour with your finger without exposing the liquid and add the yeast to it.

3 Fit the bread pan in the machine and close the lid. Set the bread machine to the basic setting, medium crust, and press start.

4 When the cycle has finished, switch off the machine. Remove the bread pan with oven gloves and turn out the bread on to a wire rack to cool. Remove the kneading blade if necessary.

PARSLEY AND CHIVE COTTAGE LOAF

INGREDIENTS

300 ml/10 fl oz hand-hot water
450 g/1 lb strong white bread flour,
    plus extra for dusting
1½ tsp salt
1½ tsp sugar
1½ tsp easy-blend dried yeast
2 tbsp chopped fresh parsley

2 tbsp chopped fresh chives
1 tbsp chopped fresh thyme
sunflower oil, for greasing

Glaze
1 tbsp water
1 tbsp salt

1 Remove the bread pan from the bread machine. Pour the water into the bread pan. Sprinkle the flour over the liquid so that it is completely covered. Place the salt and sugar in 2 corners of the pan. Make an indentation in the flour with your finger without exposing the liquid and add the yeast to it.

2 Fit the bread pan in the machine and close the lid. Set the bread machine to the dough setting. When the machine beeps, or 5 minutes before the end of kneading, add all the herbs.

3 When the cycle has finished, switch off the machine and remove the bread pan. Lightly flour 2 baking sheets and a work surface. Remove the dough from the pan. Knock back gently, then cut off one-third of the dough. Shape each piece of dough into a ball and place on the baking sheets. Cover with oiled clingfilm and set aside in a warm place for 30 minutes to rise.

4 Unwrap the dough and cut a cross in the top of the larger piece with a sharp knife. Brush with water and place the smaller piece on top. Oil the handle of a wooden spoon and push it through both balls of dough. Cover the loaf with oiled clingfilm and set aside in a warm place for 10 minutes to rise.

5 To make the glaze, pour the water into a small bowl and stir in the salt. Remove the clingfilm and brush the loaf with the glaze. Make a series of slashes around the top and bottom of the loaf with a sharp knife, and dust with flour. Bake in a preheated oven, 220°C/425°F/Gas Mark 7, for 30–35 minutes, until the loaf is golden and sounds hollow when tapped on the base. Transfer to a wire rack to cool.

CHEESY CHIVE GRANARY BREAD

INGREDIENTS

185 ml/6½ fl oz hand-hot water
1 egg, beaten lightly
5 tbsp ricotta cheese, beaten
   until smooth
55 g/2 oz Granary flour
400 g/14 oz strong white bread
   flour, plus extra for dusting
1 tsp salt
2 tsp sugar

1½ tsp easy-blend dried yeast
85 g/3 oz dolcelatte cheese,
   diced finely
85 g/3 oz freshly grated
   Emmenthal cheese
3 tbsp finely chopped fresh chives
sunflower oil, for greasing
2 tbsp freshly grated Parmesan
   cheese

1 Remove the bread pan from the bread machine. Pour the water into the bread pan and add the egg and ricotta. Sprinkle both types of flour over the liquid so that it is completely covered. Place the salt and sugar in 2 corners of the pan. Make an indentation in the flour without exposing the liquid and add the yeast to it.

2 Fit the bread pan in the machine and close the lid. Set the bread machine to the dough setting. When the machine beeps for extra ingredients, or 5 minutes before the end of kneading, add the dolcelatte, Emmenthal and chives.

3 When the cycle has finished, switch off the machine and remove the bread pan. Lightly flour a work surface and remove the dough from the pan. Knock back gently, then shape into a round, 20 cm/ 8 inches in diameter. Place on an oiled baking sheet, cover with oiled clingfilm and set aside in a warm place for 40–45 minutes to rise.

4 Remove the clingfilm. Sprinkle over the Parmesan. Bake in a preheated oven, 200°C/400°F/Gas Mark 6, for 40–45 minutes, until the loaf is golden and sounds hollow when tapped on the base. Transfer to a wire rack to cool.

NAAN WITH GARLIC AND CORIANDER

INGREDIENTS

100 ml/3½ fl oz hand-hot water
4 tbsp natural yogurt
280 g/10 oz strong white bread flour
1 garlic clove, chopped finely
1 tsp ground coriander
1 tsp salt

2 tsp clear honey
1 tbsp ghee or butter, melted, plus
  extra for brushing
1 tsp easy-blend dried yeast
sunflower oil, for greasing
1 tsp black onion seeds
1 tbsp chopped fresh coriander

1 Remove the bread pan from the bread machine. Pour the water into the bread pan and add the yogurt. Sprinkle the flour over the liquid so that it is completely covered, then sprinkle in the garlic and ground coriander. Place the salt, honey and melted ghee in 3 corners of the pan. Make an indentation in the flour with your finger without exposing the liquid and add the yeast to it.

2 Fit the bread pan in the machine and close the lid. Set the bread machine to the dough setting or pizza dough setting and press start.

3 When the cycle has finished, switch off the machine and remove the bread pan. Place 3 baking sheets in the oven to preheat to 240°C/475°F/Gas Mark 9. Lightly flour a work surface and remove the dough from the pan. Knock back gently and divide into 3 pieces. Shape each piece into a ball and cover 2 of them with oiled clingfilm.

4 Roll out the uncovered piece of dough into a teardrop shape about 8 mm/⅜ inch thick. Cover with oiled clingfilm, then roll out the other pieces of dough in turn.

5 Place the naan on the hot baking sheets and sprinkle with the onion seeds and chopped coriander. Bake for about 5 minutes, until puffed up. Place under a preheated grill for a few seconds, until beginning to brown and blister. Brush with melted ghee and serve warm.

MIXED SEED BREAD

INGREDIENTS

300 ml/10 fl oz hand-hot water
1½ tbsp sunflower oil
2 tsp lemon juice
375 g/13 oz strong white bread flour
125 g/4½ oz rye flour
1½ tbsp skimmed milk powder

1½ tsp salt
1 tbsp light brown sugar
1 tsp caraway seeds
½ tsp poppy seeds
½ tsp sesame seeds
1 tsp easy-blend dried yeast

Topping
1 egg white
1 tbsp water
1 tbsp sunflower or
   pumpkin seeds

1 Remove the bread pan from the bread machine. Pour in the water and add the sunflower oil and lemon juice. Sprinkle both types of flour over the liquid so that it is completely covered, then sprinkle in the skimmed milk powder. Place the salt, sugar and seeds in 3 corners of the pan. Make an indentation in the flour with your finger without exposing the liquid and add the yeast to it.

2 Fit the bread pan in the machine and close the lid. Set the bread machine to the basic setting, medium crust, and press start.

3 To make the topping, lightly beat the egg white with the water to make a glaze. Just before the baking cycle starts (about 2 hours after the start), brush the glaze over the loaf, then gently press the sunflower or pumpkin seeds all over the top.

4 When the cycle has finished, switch off the machine. Remove the bread pan with oven gloves and turn out the bread on to a wire rack to cool. Remove the kneading blade if necessary.

FRUIT AND NUT BREADS

Fruits and nuts give breads some wonderful textures and flavours. In this chapter, dried or fresh fruits and a variety of nuts are used to produce an appetising selection of breads, cakes and pastries that are a perfect treat at any time of the day. Why not try Marmalade Bread or Orange and Banana Bread for that fruity tang, or if you prefer a mixture of fruit and nuts, choose the Walnut and Apple Streusel? For a lovely malty bread try the Malted Fruit Loaf, while the Walnut Loaf is a sophisticated nut bread enhanced by the flavour of different herbs.

APRICOT MUESLI BREAD

INGREDIENTS

250 ml/8 fl oz hand-hot water
2 tbsp sunflower oil, plus extra
   for greasing
1 tbsp clear honey
300 g/10½ oz strong white bread flour
85 g/3 oz wholemeal bread flour, plus
   extra for dusting

150 g/5½ oz unsweetened muesli
3 tbsp skimmed milk powder
1½ tsp salt
1½ tsp easy-blend dried yeast
70 g/2½ oz ready-to-eat dried
   apricots, chopped

1 Remove the bread pan from the bread machine. Put the water, sunflower oil and honey into the bread pan. Sprinkle both types of flour over the liquid to cover it completely, then sprinkle in the muesli and skimmed milk powder. Place the salt in 1 corner of the pan. Make an indentation in the flour with your finger without exposing the liquid and add the yeast to it.

2 Fit the bread pan in the machine and close the lid. Set the bread machine to the dough setting and press start. When the machine beeps for extra ingredients, or 5 minutes before the end of kneading, add the dried apricots.

3 When the cycle has finished, switch off the machine and remove the bread pan. Lightly oil a baking sheet. Lightly dust a work surface with the wholemeal flour and remove the dough from the pan. Knock back gently, then shape into a round loaf. Place on the baking sheet. Cut a deep cross in the top with a sharp knife. Cover with lightly oiled clingfilm and set aside in a warm place for about 30–40 minutes to rise.

4 Remove the clingfilm and bake the bread in a preheated oven, 200°C/400°F/Gas Mark 6, for 30–35 minutes, until golden. Transfer to a wire rack to cool.

FIG AND ROSEMARY BREAD

INGREDIENTS

160 ml/5½ fl oz hand-hot water
2 eggs, beaten lightly
4 tbsp olive oil
500 g/1 lb 2 oz strong white
    bread flour
2 tbsp skimmed milk powder

1 tbsp finely chopped fresh rosemary
1½ tsp salt
2 tsp sugar
1 tsp easy-blend dried yeast
115 g/4 oz dried figs, chopped
    roughly

1 Remove the bread pan from the bread machine. Pour the water into the bread pan and add the eggs and olive oil.

2 Sprinkle the flour over the liquid so that it is completely covered, then sprinkle in the skimmed milk powder and the rosemary. Place the salt and sugar in 2 corners of the pan. Make an indentation in the flour with your finger without exposing the liquid and add the yeast to it.

3 Fit the bread pan in the machine and close the lid. Set the bread machine to the basic setting, medium crust, and press start. When the machine beeps for extra ingredients, or 5 minutes before the end of kneading, add the figs.

4 When the cycle has finished, switch off the machine. Remove the bread pan with oven gloves and turn out the bread on to a wire rack to cool. Remove the kneading blade if necessary.

ORANGE AND BANANA BREAD

INGREDIENTS

4 tbsp orange juice

200 ml/7 fl oz buttermilk or water

2 medium ripe bananas or 1 large ripe
banana, peeled and mashed

3 tbsp clear honey

500 g/1 lb 2 oz strong white bread
flour, plus extra 1–2 tbsp for
sticky dough

1½ tbsp skimmed milk powder,
optional

1 tsp salt

40 g/1½ oz butter, softened or diced

1 tsp easy-blend dried yeast

milk, for glazing, optional

1 Remove the bread pan from the bread machine. Pour the orange juice and hand-hot buttermilk or water into the bread pan. Add the mashed bananas and honey.

2 Sprinkle the flour over the liquid and fruit so that it is completely covered. If using water, sprinkle the skimmed milk powder over the flour, but do not add it if you have used buttermilk. Place the salt and butter in 2 corners of the bread pan. Make an indentation in the flour with your finger without exposing the liquid and add the yeast to it.

3 Fit the bread pan in the machine and close the lid. Set the bread machine to the basic setting, medium crust, and press start. If the dough looks very sticky towards the end of the first kneading, add a further 1–2 tablespoons of strong white bread flour. (The stickiness depends on the ripeness of the bananas.)

4 Just before the baking cycle starts (about 2 hours after the start), brush the top of the loaf with milk to glaze, if you like. When the cycle has finished, switch off the machine. Remove the bread pan with oven gloves and turn out the bread on to a wire rack to cool.

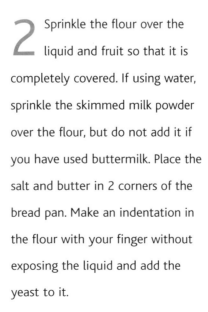

WALNUT AND APPLE STREUSEL

INGREDIENTS

100 ml/3½ fl oz hand-hot milk
1 egg, beaten lightly
250 g/9 oz strong white bread flour,
    plus extra for dusting
½ tsp salt
3 tbsp caster sugar
25 g/1 oz butter, melted
1 tsp easy-blend dried yeast
sunflower oil, for greasing

Topping

115 g/4 oz plain flour
55 g/2 oz butter, diced
55 g/2 oz walnuts, chopped finely
4 tbsp caster sugar
1 tsp ground cinnamon
4 eating apples
2 tbsp lemon juice

1 Remove the bread pan from the bread machine. Pour the milk into the bread pan and add the egg. Sprinkle the flour over the liquid so that it is completely covered. Place the salt, sugar and butter in 3 corners of the pan. Make an indentation in the flour with your finger without exposing the liquid and add the yeast to it.

2 Fit the bread pan in the machine and close the lid. Set the bread machine to the dough setting and press start. Meanwhile, make the topping. Sift the flour into a bowl and add the butter. Rub in with your fingertips until the mixture resembles coarse breadcrumbs. Stir in the walnuts, sugar and cinnamon. Set aside until required.

3 When the cycle has finished, switch off the machine. Lightly grease a round 25-cm/10-inch-diameter springform cake tin. Lightly flour a work surface and remove the dough from the pan. Knock back gently, then roll out into a round to fit the tin. Ease the dough into the tin.

4 Peel, core and thinly slice the apples. Toss them in the lemon juice to prevent them from discolouring, then arrange in circles on top of the dough. Sprinkle the nut topping over them. Cover the cake with lightly oiled clingfilm and set aside in a warm place for 25–30 minutes to rise. Remove the clingfilm and bake the cake in a preheated oven, 190°C/375°F/Gas Mark 5, for about 30 minutes, until golden. Leave in the tin to cool for 5 minutes, then transfer to a wire rack to cool completely.

CINNAMON AND APRICOT BUNS

INGREDIENTS

225 ml/7½ fl oz hand-hot milk
1 egg, beaten lightly
500 g/1 lb 2 oz strong white bread
   flour, plus extra for dusting
½ tsp salt
85 g/3 oz caster sugar
55 g/2 oz butter, softened or diced
1 tsp easy-blend dried yeast
sunflower oil, for greasing

Filling
25 g/1 oz butter, melted
115 g/4 oz ready-to-eat dried
   apricots, chopped
55 g/2 oz sultanas
2 tbsp light brown sugar
1½ tsp ground cinnamon

Glaze
4 tbsp water
4 tbsp caster sugar
1 tsp Amaretto liqueur

1 Remove the bread pan from the bread machine. Pour the milk into the bread pan and add the egg. Sprinkle the flour over the liquid so that it is completely covered. Place the salt, sugar and butter in 3 corners of the pan. Make an indentation in the flour with your finger without exposing the liquid and add the yeast to it.

2 Fit the bread pan in the machine and close the lid. Set the bread machine to the dough setting and press start. When the cycle has finished, switch off the machine and remove the bread pan. Lightly grease a 23-cm/9-inch square cake tin and lightly flour a work surface. Remove the dough from the pan and knock back gently. Roll out into a 30-cm/12-inch square. For the filling brush the surface of the dough with the melted butter, then sprinkle the apricots, sultanas, sugar and cinnamon evenly over it, leaving a 1-cm/½-inch border on one edge.

3 Roll up the dough, like a Swiss roll, from the filling-covered edge to the uncovered edge. Press firmly to seal, then cut into 12 slices. Arrange the slices in the cake tin with the cut sides upwards. Cover with lightly oiled clingfilm and set aside in a warm place for about 45 minutes to rise. Remove the clingfilm and bake the buns in a preheated oven, 200°C/400°F/Gas Mark 6, for about 20 minutes, until golden brown. Leave in the tin to cool for 5 minutes, then turn out on to a wire rack.

4 Meanwhile, make the glaze. Heat the water and sugar in a small saucepan, stirring until the sugar has dissolved. Bring to the boil, then continue to boil, without stirring, for 1½–2 minutes, until syrupy. Stir in the liqueur and brush the syrup all over the buns. Serve warm or cold.

MARMALADE BREAD

INGREDIENTS

150 ml/5 fl oz hand-hot water
150 ml/5 fl oz hand-hot milk
2 tbsp sunflower oil, plus extra
    for greasing
450 g/1 lb strong white bread flour,
    plus extra for dusting
1½ tsp salt
1½ tsp sugar

1½ tsp easy-blend dried yeast
7 tbsp orange marmalade

Topping
1 egg yolk
1 tbsp milk
1 tbsp caster sugar
1–2 tbsp crystallized orange peel

1 Remove the bread pan from the bread machine. Pour the water and milk into the bread pan and add the oil. Sprinkle the flour over the liquid so that it is completely covered. Place the salt and sugar in 2 corners of the bread pan. Make an indentation in the flour with your finger without exposing the liquid and add the yeast to it.

2 Fit the bread pan in the machine and close the lid. Set the bread machine to the dough setting and press start.

3 When the cycle has finished, switch off the machine and remove the bread pan. Lightly flour a work surface and remove the dough from the pan. Knock back gently, then roll out into a 25 x 20-cm/ 10 x 8-inch rectangle about 2 cm/ ¾ inch thick.

4 Lightly grease a 25 x 10-cm/ 10 x 4-inch loaf tin with oil. Spread the marmalade evenly over the dough, leaving a 1-cm/½-inch border on one long edge.

5 Roll up the dough like a Swiss roll, from the filling-covered edge to the uncovered edge. Press firmly to seal, and place seam-side down in the tin. Cover with lightly oiled clingfilm. Set aside in a warm place for about 45 minutes to rise to the top of the tin.

6 To make the topping, lightly beat the egg yolk with the milk and caster sugar and brush over the loaf. Score the top of the bread with 3–4 shallow, diagonal cuts. Arrange the orange peel on the loaf. Bake in a preheated oven, 220°C/425°F/Gas Mark 7, for 35–40 minutes, until golden. Transfer to a wire rack to cool.

WALNUT LOAF

INGREDIENTS
250 ml/8 fl oz hand-hot water
5 tsp sunflower oil
1½ tsp walnut oil
1½ tsp chopped basil in oil, drained
350 g/12 oz strong white bread flour
2½ tbsp skimmed milk powder
1½ tsp dried marjoram
1½ tsp dried thyme
1½ tsp salt
2¼ tbsp sugar
1¼ tsp easy-blend dried yeast
70 g/2½ oz walnuts, chopped, and
    whole walnuts for garnish

1 Remove the bread pan from the bread machine. Pour the water into the bread pan and add the sunflower oil, walnut oil and basil.

2 Sprinkle the flour over the liquid so that it is completely covered then sprinkle in the skimmed milk powder and dried herbs. Place the salt and sugar in 2 corners of the pan. Make an indentation in the flour with your finger without exposing the liquid and add the yeast to it.

3 Fit the bread pan in the machine and close the lid. Set the bread machine to the basic setting, medium crust. When the machine beeps, or 5 minutes before the end of kneading, add the chopped walnuts.

4 When the cycle has finished, switch off the machine. Remove the bread pan with oven gloves and turn out the bread on to a wire rack to cool. Top with walnuts if desired. Remove the kneading blade if necessary.

MALTED FRUIT LOAF

INGREDIENTS
225 ml/7½ fl oz hand-hot water
2 tsp sunflower oil
2 tbsp malt extract
1½ tbsp treacle
350 g/12 oz plain flour
1 tsp salt
1 tsp easy-blend dried yeast
140 g/5 oz sultanas

1 Remove the bread pan from the bread machine. Pour the water into the bread pan and add the sunflower oil, malt extract and treacle.

2 Sprinkle the flour over the liquid so that it is completely covered. Place the salt in 1 corner of the pan. Make an indentation in the flour with your finger without exposing the liquid and add the yeast to it.

3 Fit the bread pan in the machine and close the lid. Set the bread machine to basic setting, medium crust, and switch on. When the machine beeps for extra ingredients, or 5 minutes before the end of kneading, add the sultanas.

4 When the cycle has finished, switch off the machine. Remove the bread pan with oven gloves and turn out the bread on to a wire rack to cool. Remove the kneading blade if necessary.

ALMOND PASTRIES

INGREDIENTS

Danish pastry

5 tbsp hand-hot milk

2 eggs, one separated

225 g/8 oz strong white bread flour,
  plus extra for dusting

1/2 tsp salt

1 tbsp caster sugar

140 g/5 oz butter, softened

sunflower oil, for greasing

1 tbsp water

flaked almonds, for sprinkling

Filling

1 tbsp butter

85 g/3 oz caster sugar

85 g/3 oz ground almonds

2–3 drops almond essence

1 small egg, beaten lightly

1 First, make the pastry. Remove the bread pan from the bread machine. Pour the milk into the bread pan and add the whole egg. Sprinkle the flour over the liquid. Place the salt, sugar and 25 g/1 oz of the butter in 3 corners of the pan. Make an indentation in the flour with your finger without exposing the liquid and add the yeast to it. Fit the pan in the machine, close the lid, set it at dough setting and press start. Shape the butter into a 2-cm/3/4-inch-thick rectangle.

2 Roll out the finished dough into a rectangle twice as long and a little wider than the butter. Place the butter on one half of the dough rectangle, fold the other half over and seal the edges. Roll out again into a rectangle about 2 cm/3/4 inch thick, then fold the top-third down and the bottom-third up and seal the edges. Wrap in clingfilm and chill for 15 minutes. Repeat the process two more times, wrapping and chilling for 20 minutes each time.

3 To make the filling, cream the butter with the sugar until pale and fluffy. Add the ground almonds and almond essence, then stir in the beaten egg.

4 Lightly beat the white from the separated egg. Roll out the dough into a 40 x 30-cm/16 x 12-inch rectangle and cut into 10-cm/4-inch squares. Spread a little filling on half of each square, brush the edges with the egg white, fold the pastry over the filling and seal. Cut decoratively along the sealed edges and place on an oiled baking sheet. Cover with oiled clingfilm and set aside for 30 minutes to rise.

5 Beat the remaining egg yolk with the water and brush over the pastries. Sprinkle with the flaked almonds and bake in a preheated oven, 200°C/400°F/Gas Mark 6, for 15 minutes, until golden. Transfer to a wire rack to cool.

PIZZA AND MEDITERRANEAN BREADS

With a bread machine, making perfect pizza dough is simplicity itself. This chapter includes recipes for different kinds of dough. It's up to you whether you make thin-crust or thick-crust, large or individual pizzas. There is also a recipe for Roasted Vegetable Calzone, a kind of inside-out pizza. The recipes here include a selection of toppings, but you can substitute your favourite ingredients to make pizzas to suit all the family. This chapter also provides recipes for Focaccia with Mozzarella and Rosemary and the classic Provençal recipe made with olives, Pissaladière.

PEPPERONI AND ONION PIZZA

INGREDIENTS

Dough

225 ml/7½ fl oz hand-hot water

15 g/½ oz butter, melted

325 g/11½ oz strong white bread flour,
   plus extra for dusting

1 tsp salt

2 tbsp sugar

1 tsp easy-blend dried yeast

olive oil, for greasing

Topping

4 tbsp sun-dried tomato paste

4 tomatoes, skinned and sliced thinly

2 red onions, chopped finely

4 slices prosciutto or other cooked
   ham, shredded coarsely

12 slices pepperoni sausage

12 black olives

¾ tsp dried oregano or herbes
   de Provence

55 g/2 oz mozzarella cheese, grated

olive oil, for drizzling

salt

1 To make the dough, remove the bread pan from the bread machine. Pour the water into the bread pan and add the melted butter. Sprinkle the flour over the liquid so that it is completely covered. Place the salt and sugar in 2 corners of the pan. Make an indentation in the flour with your finger without exposing the liquid and add the yeast to it.

2 Fit the bread pan in the machine and close the lid. Set the bread machine to the pizza dough or dough setting. Press start.

3 When the cycle has finished, switch off the machine. Remove the bread pan. Lightly grease 2 pizza pans or baking sheets. Lightly flour a work surface and remove the dough from the pan. Knock back gently and divide in half. Roll out each piece of dough into a 25-cm/10-inch round and place on the pizza pans or baking sheets. Push up the edges slightly to make a thin rim. Cover with lightly oiled clingfilm and set aside to rest for 15 minutes.

4 To make the topping, spread the sun-dried tomato paste evenly over each pizza base. Arrange the tomato slices on each base and season with salt. Sprinkle over the chopped onion and prosciutto and arrange the pepperoni on top. Add the olives and sprinkle with oregano. Divide the grated cheese between the pizzas and drizzle with olive oil.

5 Bake in a preheated oven, 220°C/425°F/Gas Mark 7, for 20–30 minutes, until golden and sizzling. Serve immediately.

CIABATTA WITH TOMATO AND BASIL

INGREDIENTS

Italian sponge
200 ml/7 fl oz hand-hot water
175 g/6 oz strong white bread flour
½ tsp easy-blend dried yeast

Dough
200 ml/7 fl oz hand-hot water
2 tbsp olive oil, plus extra for greasing
2 tbsp milk

325 g/11½ oz strong white bread
   flour, plus extra for dusting
1½ tsp salt
½ tsp sugar
¼ tsp easy-blend dried yeast
40 g/1½ oz drained sun-dried
   tomatoes in oil, chopped roughly
   plus extra for topping if required
2 tbsp shredded fresh basil

1 Remove the bread pan from the bread machine. To make the Italian sponge, pour the water into the bread pan. Sprinkle the flour over the liquid so that it is completely covered. Make an indentation in the flour with your finger without exposing the liquid and add the yeast to it.

2 Fit the bread pan in the machine and close the lid. Set the bread machine to the dough setting and press start. After 5 minutes, switch off the machine and leave the Italian sponge in the pan for 12 hours or overnight.

3 Remove the bread pan. To make the dough, pour the water onto the sponge mixture in the bread pan. Add the olive oil and milk. Sprinkle the flour over the liquid. Place the salt and sugar in 2 corners of the pan. Make an indentation in the flour with your finger without exposing the liquid. Add the yeast.

4 Fit the bread pan in the machine and close the lid. Set the machine to the dough setting and press start. When the machine beeps, or 5 minutes before the end of kneading, add the sun-dried tomatoes and basil. When the cycle has finished, switch off the machine

and remove the bread pan. Transfer the dough to a large bowl, cover with oiled clingfilm and set aside in a warm place for 1 hour to rise.

5 Halve the dough, using a spoon, and gently tip each half on to 2 lightly floured baking sheets. Shape each piece of dough into a rectangular loaf about 2.5 cm/1 inch thick. Dust with flour and set aside, uncovered, in a warm place for 30 minutes to rise.

6 Add topping if required. Bake in a preheated oven, 220°C/ 425°F/Gas Mark 7, for 25–30 minutes, until the loaves are golden.

RICOTTA, SPINACH AND PINE KERNEL PIZZA

INGREDIENTS

Dough

300 ml/10 fl oz hand-hot water

2 tbsp olive oil, plus extra for greasing

225 g/8 oz strong white bread flour,
    plus extra for dusting

225 g/8 oz strong wholemeal
    bread flour

1¹/₂ tsp salt

¹/₂ tsp sugar

1 tsp easy-blend dried yeast

Topping `

350 g/12 oz spinach

2 tbsp olive oil, plus extra for drizzling

1 onion, sliced thinly

6 tbsp ricotta cheese

¹/₂ tsp freshly grated nutmeg

2 tbsp pine kernels

115 g/4 oz Fontina cheese,
    sliced thinly

salt and pepper

1 To make the dough, remove the bread pan from the bread machine. Pour the water into the bread pan and add the olive oil. Sprinkle both types of flour over the liquid. Place the salt and sugar in 2 corners of the pan. Make an indentation in the flour with your finger without exposing the liquid and add the yeast to it.

2 Fit the bread pan in the machine and close the lid. Set the bread machine to the pizza dough or dough setting and press start. When the cycle has finished, switch off the machine and remove the bread pan. Lightly flour a work surface and remove the dough from the pan. Knock back gently and divide in half. Roll out each piece of dough into a 30-cm/12-inch-diameter round and place on oiled pizza pans or baking sheets. Push up the edges to make a thin rim. Cover with oiled clingfilm and set aside to rest for 15 minutes.

3 To make the topping, wash the spinach in cold water and dry well. Heat the oil in a pan, add the onion and cook until soft and translucent. Add the spinach and cook, stirring, until just wilted. Remove the pan from the heat and drain off any liquid.

4 Spread the ricotta cheese evenly over the pizza bases, then cover with spinach and onion mixture. Sprinkle over the nutmeg and pine kernels and season to taste with salt and pepper. Top with the slices of Fontina and drizzle with olive oil. Bake in a preheated oven, 220°C/425°F/Gas Mark 7, for 20–30 minutes, until golden and sizzling. Serve immediately.

OLIVE AND FETA BREAD

INGREDIENTS
210 ml/7½ fl oz hand-hot water
375 g/13 oz strong white bread flour,
   plus extra for dusting
1 tbsp skimmed milk powder
1 tsp salt
1½ tsp sugar
1 tsp easy-blend dried yeast
55 g/2 oz stoned black olives,
   chopped
55 g/2 oz feta cheese, crumbled
olive oil, for brushing and greasing
mixed herbs for garnish

1 Remove the bread pan from the bread machine. Pour the water into the bread pan. Sprinkle the flour over the liquid so that it is completely covered, then sprinkle in the skimmed milk powder. Place the salt and sugar in 2 corners of the pan. Make an indentation in the flour with your finger without exposing the liquid and add the yeast to it.

2 Fit the bread pan in the machine and close the lid. Set the bread machine to the dough setting and press start. When the machine beeps, or 5 minutes before the end of kneading, add the olives and feta.

3 When the cycle has finished, switch off the machine and remove the bread pan. Lightly oil a 20-cm/8-inch-diameter round cake tin. Lightly flour a work surface and remove the dough from the pan. Knock back gently, then shape into a round, 20 cm/8 inches in diameter. Ease the dough into the cake tin, cover with lightly oiled clingfilm and set aside in a warm place for 40–45 minutes to rise.

4 Remove the clingfilm and brush the top of the loaf with olive oil. Sprinkle with herbs. Bake in a preheated oven, 200°C/400°F/Gas Mark 6, for 35–40 minutes, until the loaf is golden and sounds hollow when tapped on the base. Transfer to a wire rack to cool.

FOCACCIA WITH MOZZARELLA AND ROSEMARY

INGREDIENTS

210 ml/7½ fl oz hand-hot water
1 tbsp olive oil, plus extra for greasing
350 g/12 oz strong white bread flour,
 plus extra for dusting
½ tsp salt
1 tsp sugar

1 tsp easy-blend dried yeast
140 g/5 oz mozzarella cheese, grated

Topping
2 tbsp olive oil
fresh rosemary sprigs
coarse sea salt

1 To make the dough, remove the bread pan from the bread machine. Pour in the water and add the oil. Sprinkle the flour over the liquid. Place the salt and sugar in 2 corners of the pan. Make an indentation in the flour without exposing the liquid. Add the yeast.

2 Fit the bread pan in the machine and close the lid. Set the bread machine to the dough or pizza dough setting and press start.

3 When the cycle has finished, switch off the machine and remove the bread pan. Lightly oil a round, shallow 25-cm/10-in-diameter cake tin and flour the work surface. Remove the dough from the pan, knock back and flatten. Sprinkle over the mozzarella and knead gently to mix. Shape into a ball, flatten slightly, then roll out into a 25-cm/10-inch round. Place in the tin, cover with lightly oiled clingfilm and set aside in a warm place for 20 minutes to rise.

4 Remove the clingfilm. Make deep indentations all over the surface of the dough with your fingers. Cover with lightly oiled clingfilm and set aside in a warm place for 15 minutes to rise.

5 Remove the clingfilm. To make the topping, drizzle the olive oil all over the surface of the dough, then sprinkle with the rosemary sprigs and sea salt. Bake in a preheated oven, 200°C/400°F/Gas Mark 6, for 20–25 minutes, until golden. Transfer to a wire rack to cool slightly. Serve warm.

ROASTED VEGETABLE CALZONE

INGREDIENTS

Dough
140 ml/4½ fl oz hand-hot water
2 tbsp olive oil, plus extra for greasing
   and brushing
225 g/8 oz strong white bread flour
1 tsp salt
½ tsp sugar
1 tsp easy-blend dried yeast

Filling
1 red onion, cut into wedges
2 garlic cloves, skin left on
2 baby aubergines, quartered
   lengthways
2 courgettes, halved lengthways
1 small red pepper, deseeded and
   quartered lengthways

1 small orange pepper, deseeded and
   quartered lengthways
4 tbsp olive oil
1 tbsp balsamic vinegar
1 tbsp chopped fresh parsley
85 g/3 oz goat's cheese, diced
salt and pepper

1 To make the dough, remove the bread pan from the bread machine. Pour the water into the bread pan and add the oil. Sprinkle the flour over the liquid so that it is completely covered. Place the salt and sugar in 2 corners of the pan. Make an indentation in the flour with your finger without exposing the liquid and add the yeast to it.

2 Fit the bread pan in the machine and close the lid. Set the machine to the pizza dough or dough setting and press start.

3 When the cycle has finished, switch off the machine. Remove the bread pan. Lightly oil a large baking sheet. Lightly flour a work surface and remove the dough from the pan. Knock back gently and divide in half. Roll out each piece of dough into a round about 5 mm/¼ inch thick and place on the baking sheet. Cover with lightly oiled clingfilm and set aside to rest for 15 minutes.

4 Meanwhile, make the filling. Place the onion, garlic, aubergines, courgettes and red and orange peppers in a roasting tin. Combine the olive oil, balsamic vinegar and parsley in a bowl and season to taste with salt and pepper. Pour the oil mixture over the vegetables and toss to coat. Roast in a preheated oven, 200°C/400°F/Gas Mark 6, turning once, for about 15 minutes. Remove from the oven and set aside to cool.

5 Peel off the skins from the garlic and peppers. Divide the vegetable mixture in half. Place 1 portion of vegetables on half of each dough round, leaving a 1-cm/½-inch border. Sprinkle half of the goat's cheese over each portion of filling. Brush the edges of the dough with water, fold the uncovered halves over and seal the edges. Brush with oil and bake in a preheated oven, 220°C/425°F/Gas Mark 7, for 20–30 minutes, until golden. Serve immediately.

PISSALADIÈRE

INGREDIENTS

100 ml/3½ fl oz hand-hot water
1 egg, beaten lightly
225 g/8 oz strong white bread flour,
   plus extra for dusting
1 tsp salt
25 g/1 oz butter, softened or diced
1 tsp easy-blend dried yeast
olive oil, for greasing

Topping

3 tsp olive oil
500 g/1 lb 2 oz red onions,
   sliced thinly
2 garlic cloves, chopped finely
2 tsp caster sugar
1½ tbsp balsamic vinegar
100 g/3½ oz canned anchovy
   fillets, drained
12 black olives
1 tsp dried marjoram
salt and pepper

1 To make the dough, remove the bread pan from the bread machine. Pour the water into the bread pan and add the egg. Sprinkle the flour over the liquid so that it is completely covered. Place the salt and butter in 2 corners of the pan. Make an indentation in the flour with your finger without exposing the liquid and add the yeast to it.

2 Fit the bread pan in the machine and close the lid. Set the bread machine to the pizza dough or dough setting and press start.

3 Meanwhile, make the topping. Heat the oil in a large, heavy-based frying pan. Add the onions and garlic and cook over a low heat, stirring occasionally, for about 30 minutes, until golden. Add the sugar and vinegar and season to taste with salt and pepper. Cook, stirring frequently, for about 5 minutes, then remove the pan from the heat and set aside to cool.

4 When the cycle has finished, switch off the machine and remove the bread pan. Lightly oil a 28 x 20-cm/11 x 8-inch Swiss roll tin. Lightly flour the work surface and remove the dough from the pan. Knock back gently, then roll out into a 30 x 23-cm/12 x 9-inch rectangle. Lift the dough into the tin and ease into place so that it lines the base and sides.

5 Spread the onion mixture evenly over the base of the dough. Arrange the anchovy fillets in a criss-cross pattern on top and place the olives in between them. Sprinkle with the marjoram. Cover with lightly oiled clingfilm and set aside in a warm place for 10–15 minutes to rise.

6 Remove the clingfilm and bake in a preheated oven, 200°C/400°F/Gas Mark 6, for 25–30 minutes, until the dough is golden. Serve hot or warm.

SWEET TREATS

These delightful specialities are very easy to make using a bread machine, which produces results to rival a baker's finest confectioneries. Bake simple sweet breads such as Honey and Pecan Tea Bread in the machine, or push the boat out and make delicious Creamy Splits. Use the bread machine to mix yeast doughs to perfection before cooking in a mould or tin or shaping into buns. It is also perfect for making cakes, such as Coffee Cake with Brandy. Give yourself a mid-morning pick-me-up, take a well-deserved break with afternoon tea or simply indulge your sweet tooth at any time of day.

MUFFINS

INGREDIENTS

350 ml/12 fl oz hand-hot milk
450 g/1 lb strong white bread flour,
  or 225 g/8 oz strong white bread
  flour plus 225 g/8 oz strong
  wholemeal bread flour, plus extra
  for dusting

1½ tsp salt
1 tsp caster sugar
15 g/½ oz butter, softened or diced
1½ tsp easy-blend dried yeast
ground rice or rice flour, for dusting
sunflower oil, for greasing

1 Remove the bread pan from the bread machine. Pour the milk into the pan. Sprinkle the flour over the liquid so that it is completely covered. Place the salt, sugar and butter in 3 corners of the pan. Make an indentation in the flour with your finger without exposing the liquid and add the yeast to it.

2 Fit the bread pan in the machine and close the lid. Set the bread machine to the dough setting and press start.

3 When the cycle has finished, switch off the machine and remove the bread pan. Lightly flour a work surface and remove the dough from the pan. Knock back gently, then roll out to 1 cm/½ inch thick. Stamp out rounds with a 7.5-cm/ 3-inch plain pastry cutter. Gather up the trimmings, knead together and leave to rest for 3–4 minutes. Re-roll and stamp out another 1 or 2 muffins.

4 Dust a baking sheet with ground rice and place the muffins on it. Dust the tops with ground rice. Cover with oiled clingfilm and set aside in a warm place for 20–25 minutes to rise.

5 Remove the clingfilm. Oil a griddle pan or heavy frying pan and heat well. Cook the muffins in batches, over a low heat, for 6–7 minutes on each side. Serve warm.

HONEY AND PECAN TEA BREAD

INGREDIENTS

125 ml/4 fl oz hand-hot milk
175 ml/6 fl oz mandarin or orange
   yogurt, at room temperature
3 tbsp clear honey
500 g/1 lb 2 oz strong white
   bread flour
³/₄ tsp salt
40 g/1½ oz butter, softened or diced
1½ tsp easy-blend yeast
40 g/1½ oz pecan nuts, chopped
1 tbsp grated orange rind, optional

1 Remove the bread pan from the bread machine. Pour the milk into the bread pan and add the yogurt and honey.

2 Sprinkle the flour over the liquid so that it is completely covered. Place the salt and butter in 2 corners of the pan. Make an indentation in the flour with your finger without exposing the liquid and add the yeast to it.

3 Fit the bread pan in the machine and close the lid. Set the bread machine to the basic setting, medium crust, and press start. When the machine beeps for extra ingredients, or 5 minutes before the end of kneading, add the pecan nuts and orange rind, if using.

4 When the cycle has finished, switch off the machine. Remove the bread pan with oven gloves and turn out the bread on to a wire rack to cool. Remove the kneading blade if necessary.

CREAMY SPLITS

INGREDIENTS

150 ml/5 fl oz hand-hot milk
225 g/8 oz strong white bread flour,
   plus extra for dusting
½ tsp salt
2 tbsp caster sugar
1 tsp easy-blend dried yeast

sunflower oil, for greasing
icing sugar, for dusting

Filling
strawberry jam
double cream, whipped stiffly,
   or clotted cream

1 Remove the bread pan from the bread machine. Pour the milk into the pan. Sprinkle the flour over the liquid so that it is completely covered. Place the salt and sugar in 2 corners of the pan. Make an indentation in the flour with your finger without exposing the liquid and add the yeast to it.

2 Fit the bread pan in the machine and close the lid. Set the bread machine to the dough setting and press start.

3 When the cycle has finished, switch off the machine and remove the bread pan. Lightly oil 2 baking sheets. Lightly flour a work surface, remove the dough from the pan and knock back gently.

4 Divide the dough into 8 equal pieces and shape each one into a ball with your hands. Place on the baking sheets and flatten the tops slightly. Cover with lightly oiled clingfilm and set aside in a warm place for about 45 minutes to rise.

5 Remove the clingfilm and bake the buns in a preheated oven, 220°C/425°F/Gas Mark 7, for about 15 minutes, until golden. Transfer to a wire rack to cool completely.

6 When the buns are cold, cut them open and fill with strawberry jam and cream. Dust with icing sugar and serve.

COFFEE CAKE WITH BRANDY

INGREDIENTS

5 tbsp strong black coffee
2 tbsp brandy
1 cinnamon stick
115 g/4 oz raisins
2 tbsp hand-hot milk
3 eggs
500 g/1 lb 2 oz strong white
    bread flour

½ tsp salt
85 g/3 oz caster sugar
2 tsp easy-blend dried yeast
85 g/3 oz butter, melted,
    plus extra for greasing
sunflower oil, for greasing
2 egg whites
icing sugar, for dusting

1 Pour the coffee into a small saucepan, add the brandy and the cinnamon stick. Heat to just below boiling point, then remove from the heat. Add the raisins and set aside for 30 minutes, until the raisins have plumped up and the liquid has cooled to hand-hot.

2 Remove the bread pan from the bread machine. Pour the milk into the bread pan and strain in the coffee mixture. Discard the cinnamon stick and reserve the raisins. Add the whole eggs to the pan. Sprinkle the flour over the liquid so that it is completely covered. Place the salt and sugar in 2 corners of the pan. Make an indentation in the flour with your finger without exposing the liquid and add the yeast to it.

3 Fit the bread pan in the machine and close the lid. Set the bread machine to the dough setting and press start. After 5 minutes, add one-third of the melted butter, then close the lid. After 10 minutes, add half of the melted butter. After 15 minutes, add all the remaining butter.

4 When the cycle has finished, switch off the machine. Remove the bread pan and turn out the dough into a large mixing bowl. Gently knead in the reserved raisins.

Grease a large brioche mould with butter. Whisk the egg whites in a grease-free bowl into soft peaks. Gradually incorporate the egg whites into the dough, folding in gently. Spoon the dough into the brioche mould, cover with oiled clingfilm and set aside in a warm place for 1¼–1½ hours to rise.

5 Remove the clingfilm and bake in a preheated oven, 190°C/375°F/Gas Mark 5, for 55–60 minutes, until the surface is firm to the touch and a skewer inserted into the cake comes out clean. Turn the cake out on to a wire rack to cool, then dust with icing sugar before serving.

SAFFRON HONEY BREAD

INGREDIENTS

1 tsp saffron threads
200 ml/7 fl oz milk
2 eggs, beaten lightly
500 g/1 lb 2 oz strong white bread
   flour, plus extra for dusting
1/2 tsp salt

4 tbsp caster sugar
55 g/2 oz butter, melted
1 tsp easy-blend dried yeast
sunflower oil, for greasing

Glaze
1–2 tbsp clear honey

1 Place the saffron threads in a small bowl. Heat 5 tablespoons of the milk in a small saucepan, pour it over the saffron and set aside for at least 30 minutes.

2 Remove the bread pan from the bread machine. Pour the saffron milk and remaining unflavoured milk into the pan and add the eggs. Sprinkle the flour over the liquid so that it is completely covered. Place the salt, sugar and butter in 3 corners of the pan. Make an indentation in the flour with your finger without exposing the liquid and add the yeast to it.

3 Fit the bread pan in the machine and close the lid. Set the bread machine to the dough setting and press start.

4 When the cycle has finished, switch off the machine and remove the bread pan. Lightly oil a baking sheet. Lightly flour a work surface and remove the dough from the pan. Knock back gently, then divide into 2 pieces. Roll each piece of dough into a rope about 46 cm/18 inches long. Place the ropes side by side and, starting at the centre, twist 1 rope of dough around the other. Continue twisting until you reach the ends. Turn the dough around and twist the ropes at

the other end. Dampen the ends with water and tuck them under the loaf to seal.

5 Place the loaf on the baking sheet, cover with oiled clingfilm and set aside in a warm place for about 1 hour to rise.

6 Heat the honey for the glaze until it is runny. Remove the clingfilm and brush the top of the loaf with the honey. Bake in a preheated oven, 190°C/375°F/Gas Mark 5, for 20 minutes. Lower the oven temperature to 180°C/350°F/Gas Mark 4 and bake for a further 10–15 minutes, until golden. Transfer to a wire rack to cool.

CINNAMON AND SPICE BREAD

INGREDIENTS
350 g/12 oz plain flour
1¹⁄₂ tsp baking powder
¹⁄₄ tsp salt
1 tsp ground cinnamon
¹⁄₂ tsp mixed spice
¹⁄₂ tsp freshly grated nutmeg
¹⁄₂ tsp ground ginger
55 g/2 oz butter
4 tbsp treacle
3 eggs, beaten lightly
50 ml/2 fl oz milk
25 g/1 oz raisins
55 g/2 oz dried apple rings, snipped
    into pieces

1 Sift the flour, baking powder, salt and spices into a mixing bowl and set aside.

2 Put the butter and treacle into a saucepan over a low heat, stirring constantly, until the butter has melted. Leave to cool slightly, then stir in the eggs, milk, raisins and apple pieces. Add the treacle mixture to the flour mixture and stir gently until combined.

3 Remove the bread pan from the bread machine. Turn the mixture into the bread pan, fit the pan in the machine and close the lid. Set the bread machine to the cake setting and press start.

4 When the cycle has finished, switch off the machine. Remove the bread pan with oven gloves and turn out the bread on to a wire rack to cool. Remove the kneading blade if necessary.

PAINS AUX CHOCOLAT

INGREDIENTS

125 ml/4 fl oz hand-hot water

250 g/9 oz strong white bread flour

2 tbsp skimmed milk powder

½ tsp salt

1 tbsp caster sugar

140 g/5 oz butter, softened, plus extra
   for greasing

1½ tsp easy-blend dried yeast

sunflower oil, for greasing

225 g/8 oz plain chocolate,
   broken into pieces

Glaze

1 egg yolk

1 tsp milk

1 Remove the pan from the bread machine. Pour in the water. Sprinkle the flour over the liquid, then sprinkle in the milk powder. Place the salt, sugar and 25 g/1 oz of the butter in 3 corners of the pan. Make an indentation in the flour with your finger and add the yeast to it. Fit the pan in the machine, close the lid, set at dough setting and press start. Shape the remaining butter into a rectangle about 2 cm/¾ inch thick.

2 Knock the finished dough back gently. Shape into a ball and cut a cross in the centre halfway down through the dough. Roll out the edges of the dough, leaving the cross untouched. Place the butter rectangle in the centre and fold the rolled-out edges over it, pressing to seal. Roll out the dough again into a long rectangle. Fold the top-third of dough down and the bottom-third up and seal the edges. Wrap the dough in oiled clingfilm and chill in the refrigerator for 20 minutes. Repeat twice more, rolling from the left-hand edge each time, and finally chill for 30 minutes.

3 Roll out the dough into a 53 x 30-cm/21 x 12-inch rectangle. Cut lengthways into 3 strips, then widthways to make 9 equal rectangles. Place a few chocolate pieces on the short end of each rectangle. Beat the egg yolk with the milk and brush the glaze around the edges of the dough. Roll up the dough to enclose the chocolate and seal the edges. Transfer to oiled baking sheets, seam-side down. Cover with oiled clingfilm and set aside in a warm place for 30 minutes to rise.

4 Remove the clingfilm and brush the tops of the pastries with the remaining glaze. Bake in a preheated oven, 200°C/400°F/Gas Mark 6, for 15 minutes, until golden. Transfer to a wire rack. Serve warm.

INDEX